TAKE TEN

TAKE TEN

THE ADULT TIMEOUT
FOR RELATIONSHIPS

Cynthia Chauvin
with *Miles Chauvin*

TAKE TEN

The Adult Timeout For Relationships

ISBN 13: 978-0-9816467-4-9

Cover and Interior Design by Nu-ImageDesign.com

Cover photography: Rubberball

Author photography: Joe Henson

Bebas font courtesy: Ryoichi Tsunekawa

Published by:

Two Dragons International Inc.

Washington D.C. | New Orleans

www.twodragons.com

For special pricing on bulk sales contact

booksales@twodragons.com

For more information and companion audio products please visit

Cynthia's website:

www.cynthiachauvin.com

FOREWORD

My wife Cynthia has done thousands of psychic readings and hypnosis sessions for her clients. The insights in *Take Ten* come from these experiences.

This book, along with its companion book *The 10 Ways* and our audio CDs are all designed to empower you to create better relationships every day.

With the audio CDs, such as *Door of Transformation* and *The Golden Bubble* you can sit back and relax and take a journey. *The 10 Ways* requires you to read and be more active.

Take Ten is for quick insight when you need it most. Whether used together, or separately, this information will help you have better relationships with others by first having a better relationship with yourself.

Miles Chauvin

INTRODUCTION

The power to change lies in the ability to interrupt the patterns in our lives and replace them with a broader perspective.

Take Ten was created to be a pattern interrupter, a simple yet effective way to take the moment before a behavior is repeated and instead fill that moment with insight.

These insights allow you to rethink your present course of action thereby opening you to more choices.

Every behavior pattern you have created, most of them from childhood, started out with a base positive intent to protect you. The tools may be antiquated and no longer work to help you, but the intent still holds true.

There is a saying: Change the structure of the experience and you change the experience.

When you see new choices on how to experience a situation, you change your experience. Once an experience is changed, behavior is changed and thereby the outcome changes.

Changes are ecological. When you change one tiny part everything else starts to align itself with that new part. There is no such thing as a small change – it all has a big impact.

Relationships aren't 50/50 - they are 100/100.

You are NEVER responsible for another person's behavior - never – these insights are simply to help you with your 100.

HOW TO USE THIS BOOK

The idea is of this book is to literally take ten.

When you feel yourself drifting into a sea of depleting, derogatory or unsuccessful repetitive behavior take the book out and think to your self:

"What am I trying to see at this moment? How does this experience want to help me?"

Then flip to a page.

Drink the insight in and let it propagate and inform your thoughts about the situation you are dealing with.

"

One person's logic is another person's insanity.

"

"

Do not value yourself by another person's opinion of you, or you will be valued by what they think of themselves.

"

"

D on't disguise your criticism
as opinion.

"

"

It is not "Why me, why me?"
It is, "What did I choose, and
what do I want to do with it?"

"

"

Don't waste your time trying to figure out what he meant. Spend your time figuring out what you meant.

"

"

We fear listening to other people's feelings because we may need to change our behavior.

"

"

Commit to life: not a person, environment, or any other segmented condition.

"

"

Things fall apart to get bigger.

"

"

I am the cause and effect of my life.

"

"

The most unappealing part of any conversation is witnessing our own behavior in another person.

"

"

Approval is the single most addictive drug.

"

"

If you must get your point across, then it was never the point that was important, but your ego.

"

"

S eek approval and you will seek criticism.

,,

"

Repetitive angry behavior is boring. If we saw it in a movie theater we would walk out.

"

"

If you find a fault, look a little deeper until the fault becomes a quality.

"

"

There is no criticism without belief in what was said.

"

"

There are no reasons; just excuses we make reasons.

"

"

The wounds of the heart fester until we have seen the events through the eyes of the other.

"

"

We utilize our environment to excuse our behavior.

"

"

Memory is amazing; it contorts itself to justify today's feeling.

"

"

Acquiescence is not acceptance.

"

"

Yes is not acceptance. No is not rejection.

"

"

E motions are like children. If you give yourself over to them, they will rule you. If you parent them and see them in a bigger perspective, they'll grow.

"

"

Attach yourself to an outcome, and you sink your boat of choices.

"

"

Should or should not are just guilt; will or will not is just choice.

"

"

Fighting over anything creates control over you.

"

"

The only thing that keeps us from relating to one another is how defiant we are against knowing ourselves.

"

"

Vulnerability is strength. The rest is weakness.

"

"

The more you grow; the less you need to know.

"

"

The greatest fear is change, and the only inevitable thing is change.

"

"

Staying present is like driving a car; look too far in any direction and you lose the road.

"

"

There are a thousand languages to say things in, and a million ways to relate, but only one we understand; our own.

"

"

Reactions are the choices of an immature ego.

"

"

When we are in the world of approval, we hear nothing that is real.

"

"

When we try to change our behavior and not its attachment to an outcome, we have just treated the effect and not recognized the cause.

"

"

You can hang on out of fear, or let go out of fear, both are two sides of the same coin.

"

"

There is an opinion to support every judgment, and a judgment to support every opinion.

"

"

If you need to be heard, then you are not listening to yourself.

"

"

Until we see our qualities clearly we will criticize others.

"

"

No one can manipulate you
without your complicity.

"

"

Bring yourself into focus. Clean the lens through which you see yourself.

"

"

Those who do not think themselves worthy of receiving create expectations of others.

"

CYNTHIA CHAUVIN

"

When one over-reacts to a situation, it rarely has anything to do with what is currently happening.

"

"

We all live on the planet narcissism.

"

"

If it comes out of your mouth it is about you. If it comes out of his mouth it is about him. If you have a feeling about what comes out of his mouth it is about you.

"

"

You can't relate to another person when you are over identified with them for your safety, value or authority.

"

"

You can't leave your issues by leaving a relationship or by avoiding one.

"

"

Excuses carry guilt. Reasons carry information.

"

"

Don't look at a man's brain and try to make a woman's logic.

"

"

P erceptions stand in the way
of clarity.

"

"

Words without action are empty. Actions without words are meaningless.

"

"

Never react to what you see, respond to what you know.

"

Be the center of your world then you will center your world.

"

"

What you are consciously fighting, you have subconsciously chosen.

"

"

You need to come into the present or you will be living your past in your future.

"

"

If you can't see the potential in another you can't see the potential in yourself.

"

"

D on't get lost in the illusions
of your conclusions.

"

"

What disappoints us about people is not the people, but the expectations we have of them.

"

"

Don't let your expectations keep you from happiness.

"

"

We do not gain our freedom by leaving a relationship, but by creating a relationship with ourselves.

"

"

The only time we understand another person's creation is when we understand our own.

"

"

Your observation changes your reality.

"

"

The most liberating choice you can make is curiosity.

"

"

There is only one single, constant thread to all of your experiences: YOU.

"

"

You can't build a new relationship from old thoughts about yourself and expect a different outcome.

"

"

There is no why that will satisfy when it does not come from curiosity.

"

"

C hildren scream for attention –good or bad.

"

"

There is no ability to say yes without the ability to say no.

"

"

To own your behavior empowers you with choice.

"

"

A curious why is a productive why.

"

"

G ood communication begins
with self-communication.

"

"

Do you have a commitment to non-commitment?

"

"

You can always take the time to think about what you want to say and to see a situation clearly, but you can't take back the time when you don't.

"

"

If I say nothing, the something becomes obvious.

"

"

Fighting is the ultimate projection.

"

"

Giving is complete and onto itself, it needs no reward.

"

"

If you manipulate you will be manipulated.

"

"

F inding yourself in any given
situation is never your fault,
just your choice.

"

"

It is easier to live in need than to be disappointed by hopes.

"

"

Everybody pretends to be something until they know who they are.

"

"

C ommit to life, not a person, environment, or any other segmented condition.

"

"

P eople are not our creators; they are simply a reflection of what we create.

"

"

Consciousness flows like a river. Sometime we dam this river with denial.

"

"

Whatever is given with the heart is big. Whatever is given from the pocket is small.

"

"

We fear making a decision to the point where fear is our decision.

"

"

T ake your history and educate yourself from it, do not limit yourself with it.

"

"

L ife is not a negotiation with other people, but a negotiation with our selves.

"

"

I can't do what I am supposed to do until you do what I think you are supposed to do. This is the most common excuse not to change.

"

"

To discover, one must have no direction and no desired outcome, just curiosity. Discover the moment.

"

"

L ife is an attitude. Pick one and have it all day. Remember, it will change tomorrow.

"

"

Adults move beyond; children seek revenge.

"

"

Once you notice some aspect of yourself it can no longer sleep.

"

"

Memory is amazing: it contorts itself to justify today's feelings.

"

"

E very time you are afraid
of an ending you are afraid
of a beginning.

"

"

People are very accepting until they actually have to accept something they don't like.

"

"

We cannot change the past except by the way we experience it today.

"

"

It is amazing what happens when you start experiencing your life instead of being possessed by it.

"

"

We fight and destroy when there is no communication.

"

"

The integrity of a relationship rests in the acceptance of each other.

"

"

Change comes when we feel our feelings without being afraid of the outcome.

"

"

Consciousness is observation, then participation—not participation, then observation.

"

"

Capture the moment and you dispel the illusion.

"

"

Decisions made from your emotions are like a five-year-old driving your car.

"

"

L ove not put into action is not
love.

"

"

We do what we see, until we see what we do.

"

"

Keep the focus on the joy in your day and the joy in your life will unfold.

"

"

When you don't feel safe in your own being you won't feel safe with someone else.

"